Easy Piano CD Play-Along

Volume 20

Orchestrated arrangements with you as the soloist!

INCLUDES CD

ANDREW LLOYD WEBBER™ FAVORITES

T0082050

Andrew Lloyd Webber™ is a trademark owned by Andrew Lloyd Webber

ISBN 978-1-4234-5801-2

HAL•LEONARD®
CORPORATION

7777 W. BLUEMOUND RD. P.O. BOX 13819 MILWAUKEE, WI 53213

Visit Hal Leonard Online at
www.halleonard.com

AMIGOS PARA SIEMPRE
(Friends for Life)
(The Official Theme of the Barcelona 1992 Games)

Music by ANDREW LLOYD WEBBER
Lyrics by DON BLACK

Gentle Habanera feel

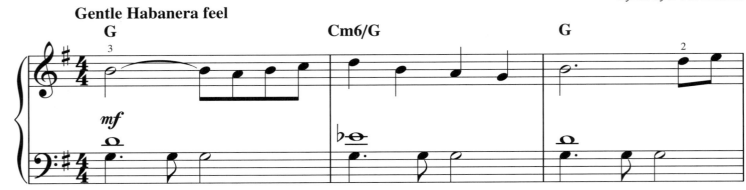

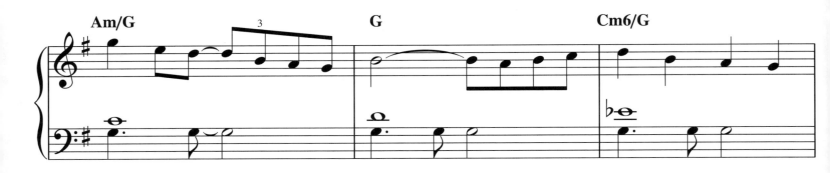

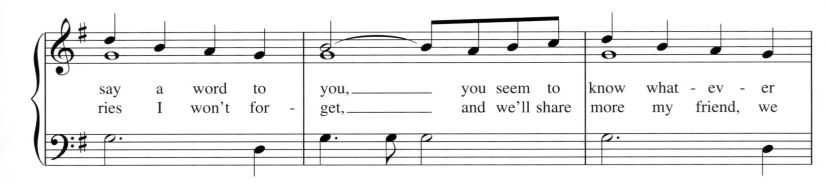

I_____ don't have to
We_____ share mem - o -

say a word to you,_____ you seem to know what - ev - er
ries I won't for - get,_____ and we'll share more my friend, we

mood I'm go - ing through,
have - n't start - ed yet.

feel as though I've known you for - ev -
Some - thing hap - pens when we're to - geth -

\- er.
\- er.

You_____ can look in -
When_____ I look at

to my eyes and see_____ the way I feel and how the
you, I won - der why_____ there has to come a time when

world is treat - ing me.
we must say good - bye.

May - be I have known you for - ev -
I'm a - live when we are to - geth -

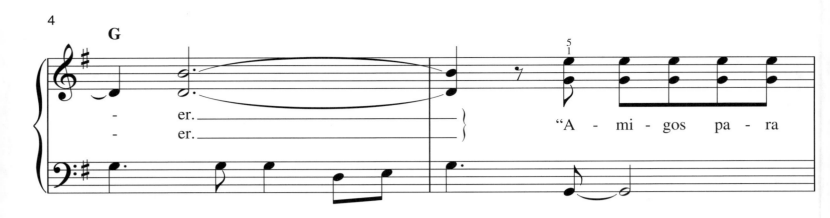

- er. _____ "A - mi - gos pa - ra
- er. _____

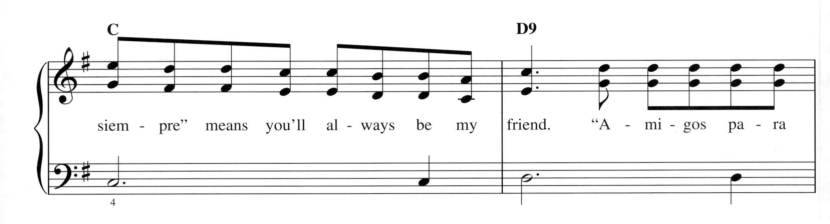

siem - pre" means you'll al - ways be my friend. "A - mi - gos pa - ra

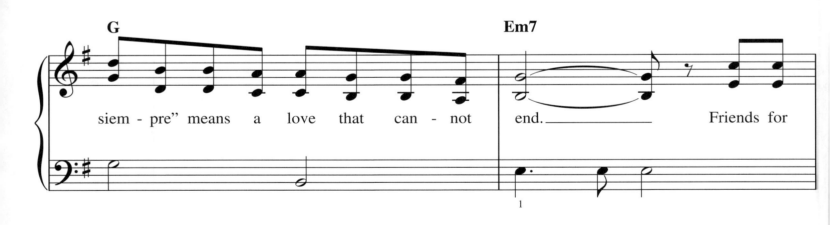

siem - pre" means a love that can - not end. _____ Friends for

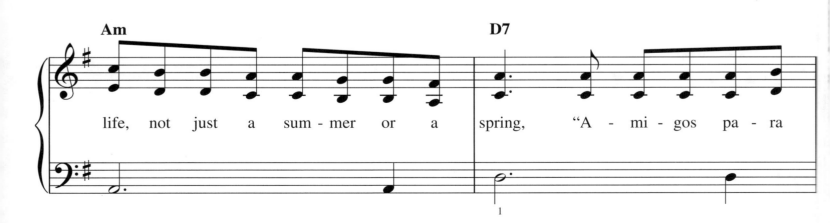

life, not just a sum - mer or a spring, "A - mi - gos pa - ra

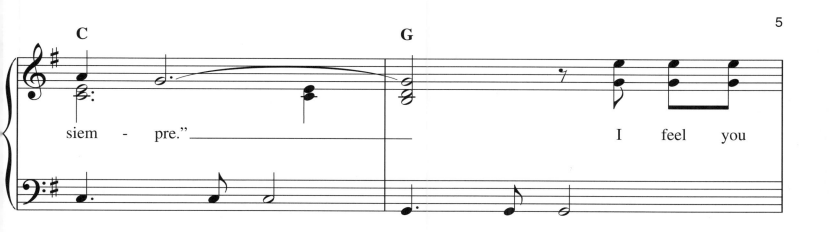

siem - pre." I feel you

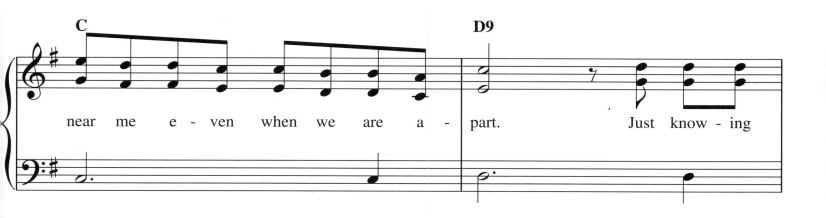

near me e - ven when we are a - part. Just know - ing

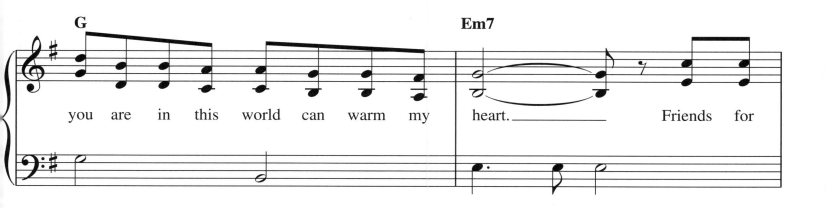

you are in this world can warm my heart. Friends for

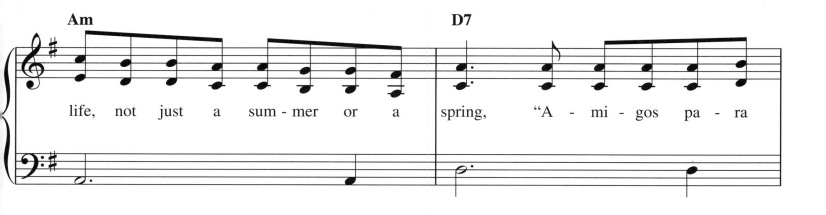

life, not just a sum - mer or a spring, "A - mi - gos pa - ra

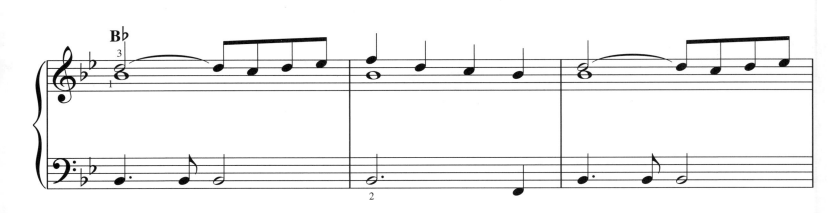

siem - pre."

When_____ I look at

you, I won-der why_____ there has to come a time when

we must say good-bye.   I'm a - live when we are to-geth - er._____

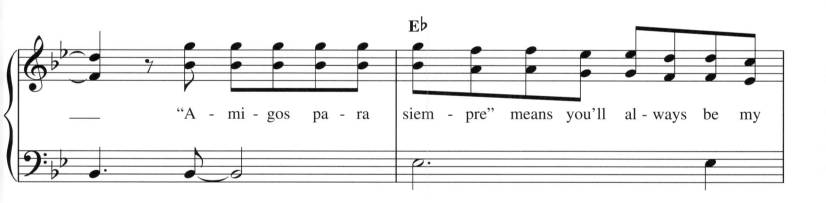

_____ "A - mi - gos pa - ra   siem - pre" means you'll al - ways be my

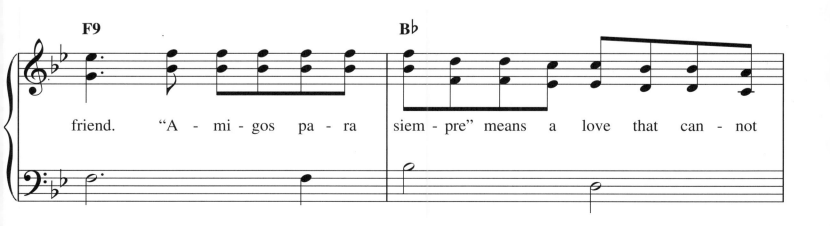

friend.   "A - mi - gos pa - ra   siem - pre" means a love that can - not

end._____ Friends for | life, not just a sum-mer or a | spring, "A - mi-gos pa - ra

siem - pre."_____ | I feel you | near me e - ven when we are a-

part. Just know-ing | you are in this world can warm my | heart._____ Friends for

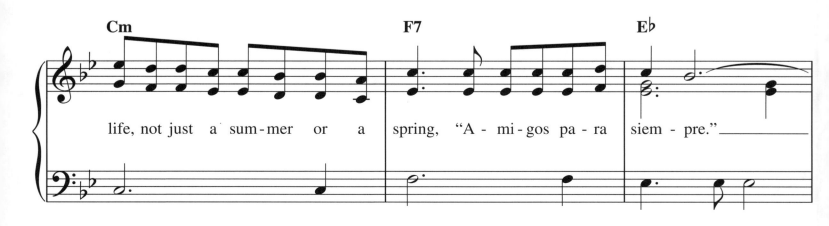

life, not just a' sum-mer or a | spring, "A - mi-gos pa - ra | siem - pre."_____

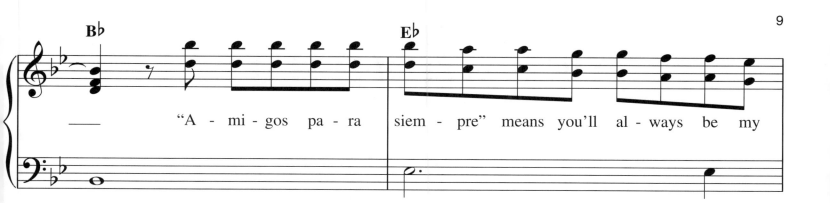

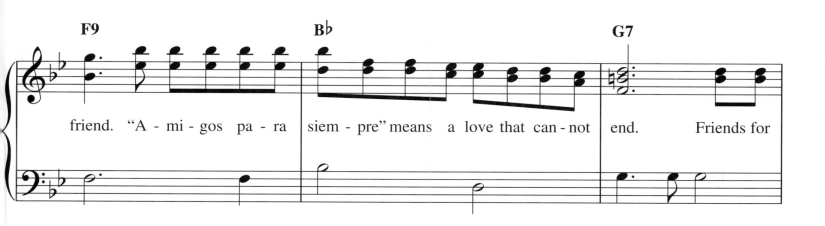

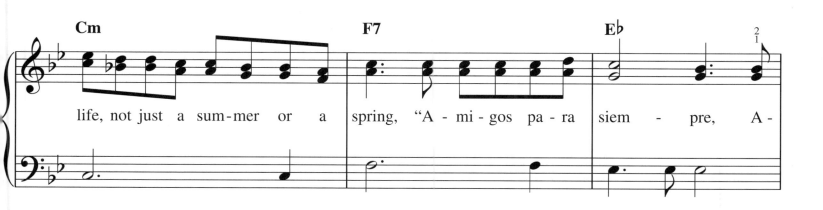

ANOTHER SUITCASE IN ANOTHER HALL

from EVITA

Words by TIM RICE
Music by ANDREW LLOYD WEBBER

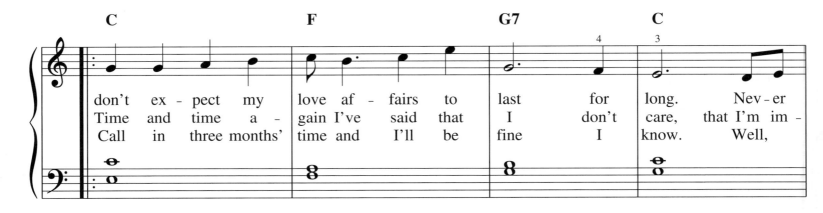

don't ex - pect my love af - fairs to last for long. Nev - er
Time and time a - gain I've said that I don't care, that I'm im -
Call in three months' time and I'll be fine I know. Well,

fool my - self that my dreams will come
mune to gloom, that I'm hard through and
maybe not that fine, but I'll sur - vive an - y -

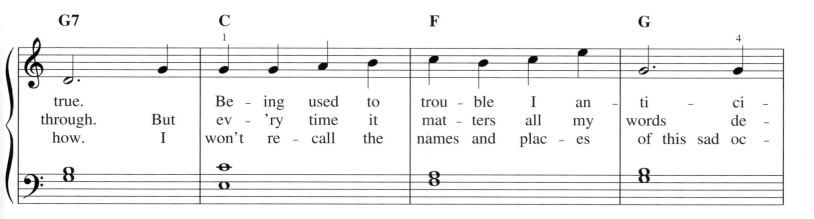

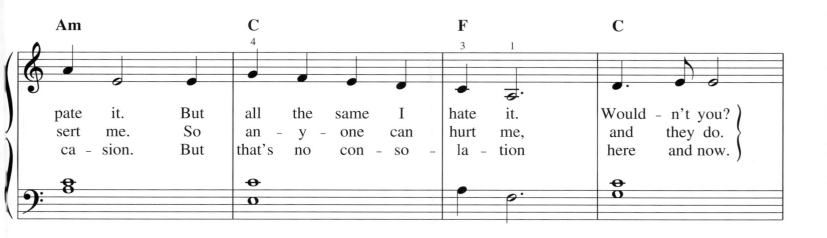

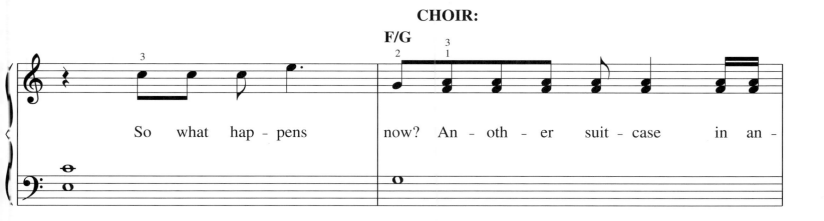

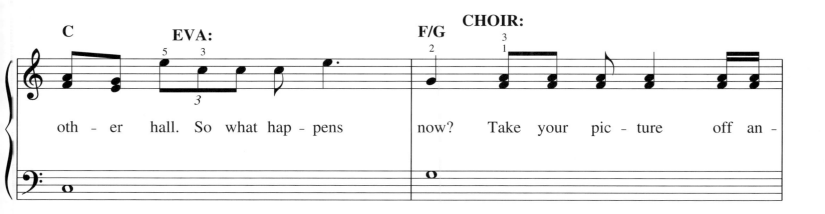

12

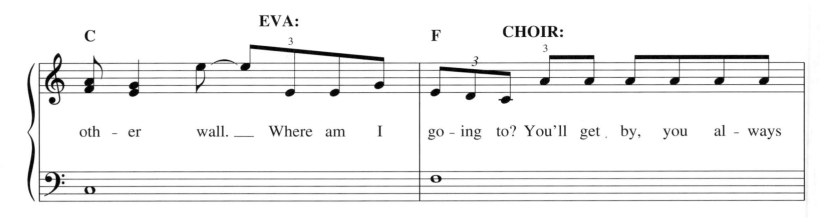

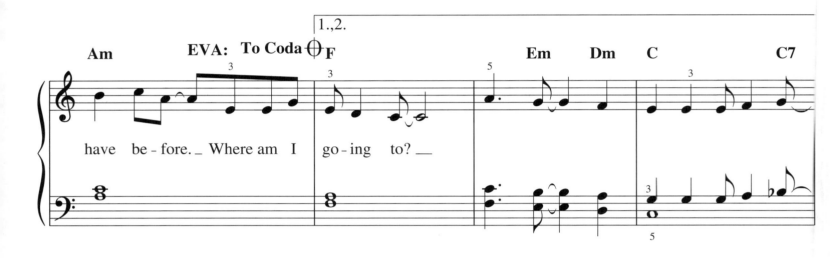

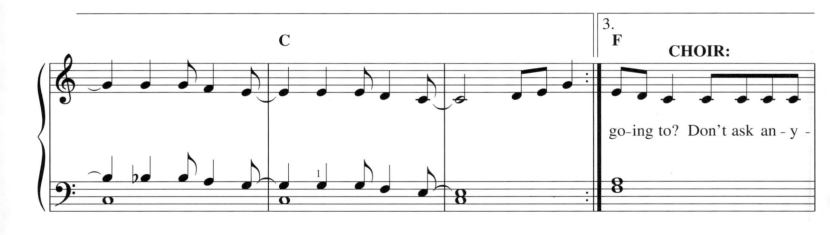

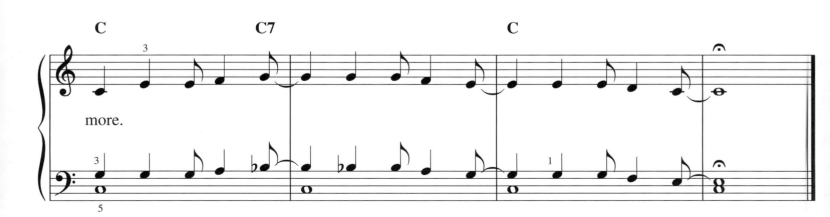

AS IF WE NEVER SAID GOODBYE
from SUNSET BOULEVARD

Music by ANDREW LLOYD WEBBER
Lyrics by DON BLACK and CHRISTOPHER HAMPTON,
with contributions by AMY POWERS

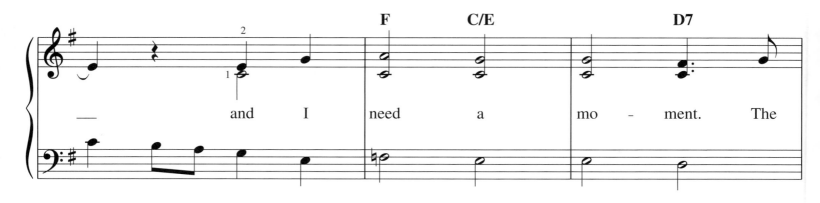

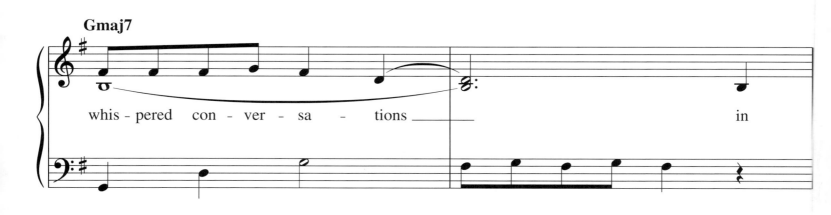

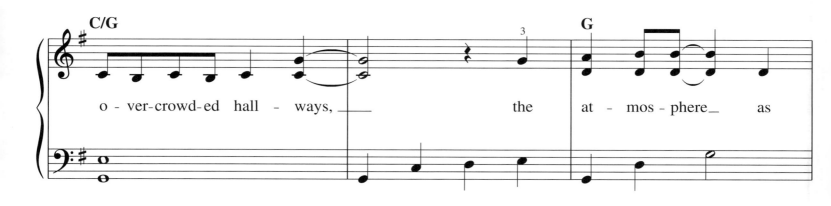

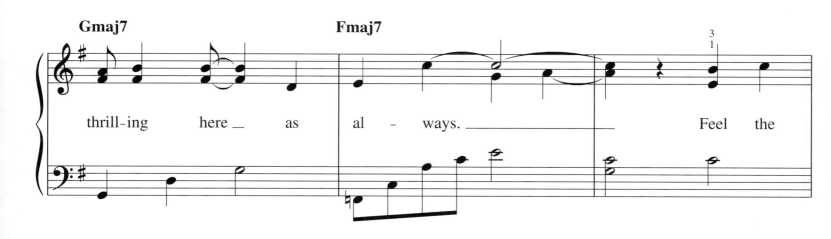

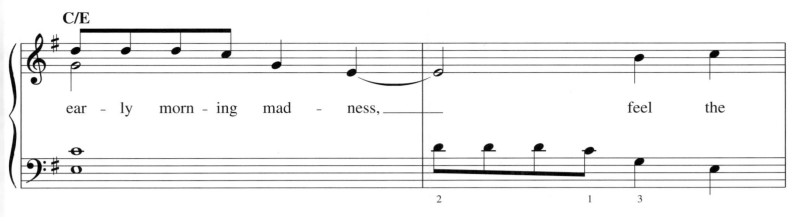

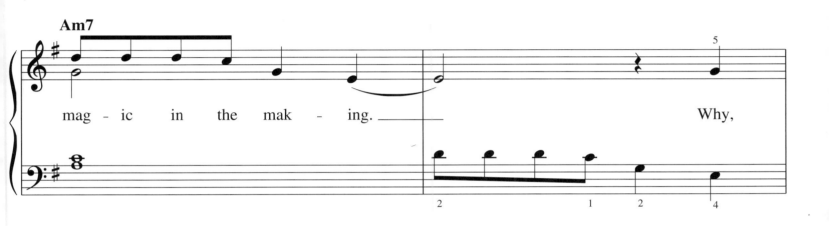

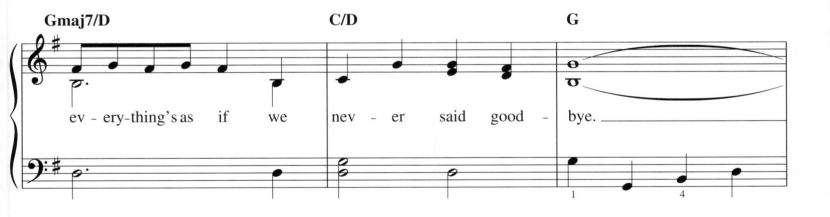

C/G — try-ing to re-sist you,_____ I'm **G** trem-bling now,__ you

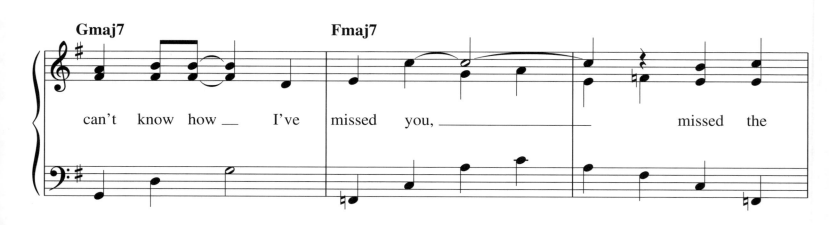

Gmaj7 can't know how __ I've **Fmaj7** missed you,_____ missed the

C/E fair-y tale ad-ven-tures _____ in this **Am7** ev-er-spin-ning play - ground.__

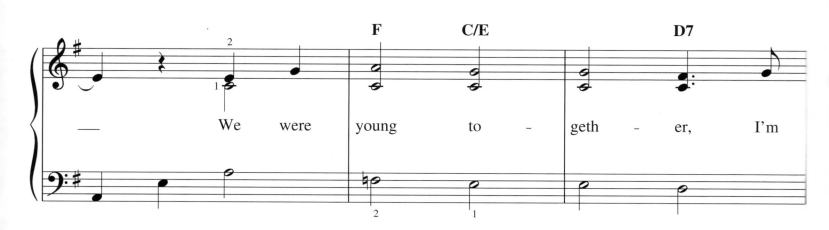

__ We were **F** young to- **C/E** geth - er, **D7** I'm

com-ing out of make - up, _____ the light's al -read - y burn - ing, _____

_____ not long un - til ___ the cam - eras will _ start

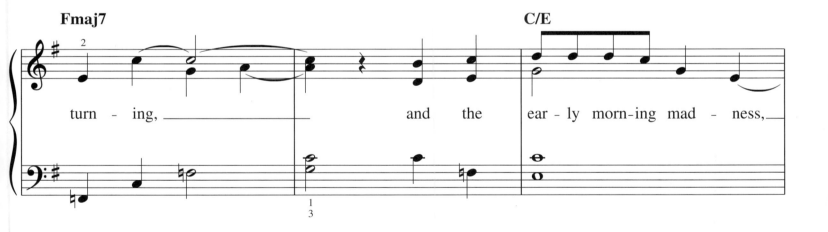

turn - ing, _____ and the ear - ly morn-ing mad - ness, ___

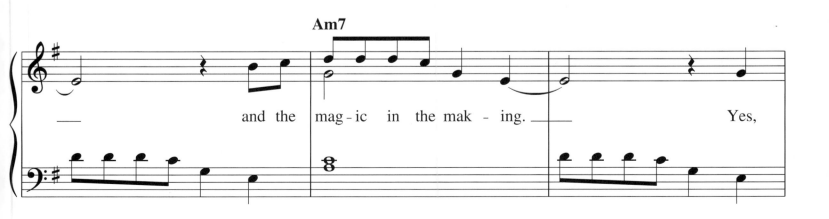

_____ and the mag - ic in the mak - ing. ___ Yes,

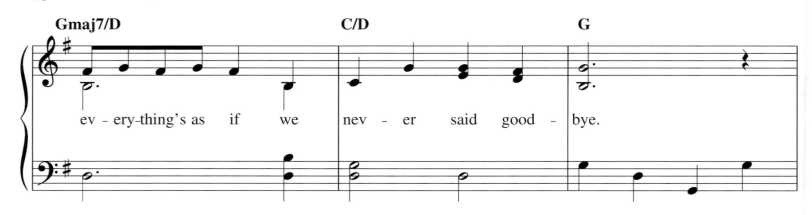

Gmaj7/D   **C/D**   **G**

ev - ery-thing's as if we nev - er said good - bye.

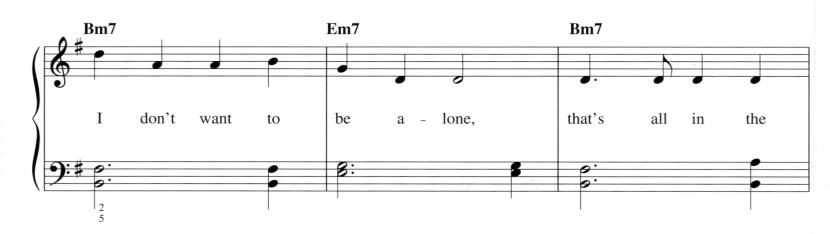

Bm7   **Em7**   **Bm7**

I don't want to be a - lone, that's all in the

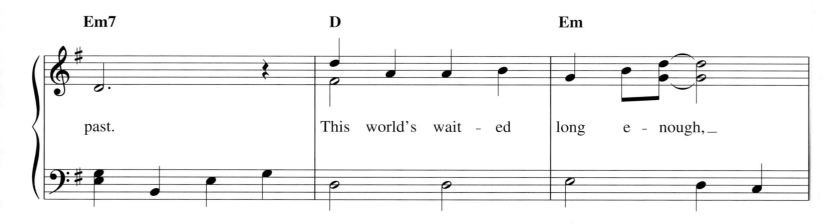

Em7   **D**   **Em**

past. This world's wait - ed long e - nough, __

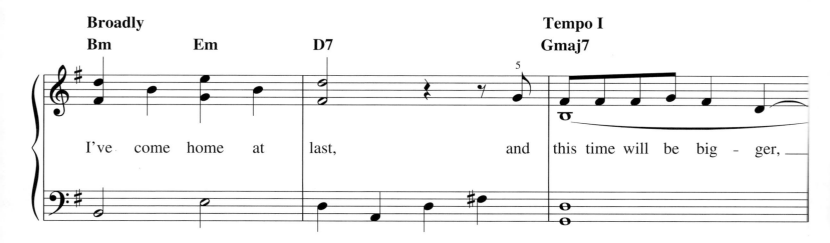

Broadly   **Tempo I**

Bm   **Em**   **D7**   **Gmaj7**

I've come home at last, and this time will be big - ger, __

and bright-er than we knew it._____ So

watch me fly,___ we all know I ___ can do it._____

___ Could I stop my hand from shak - ing?____ Has there

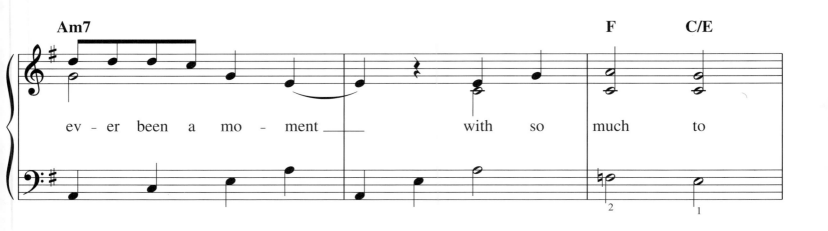

ev - er been a mo - ment ____ with so much to

live for? The whis-pered con - ver - sa - tions ___ in

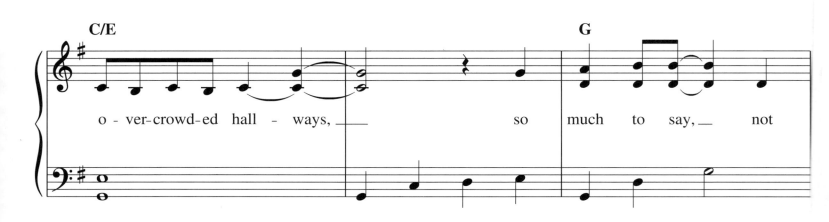

o - ver-crowd-ed hall - ways, ___ so much to say, ___ not

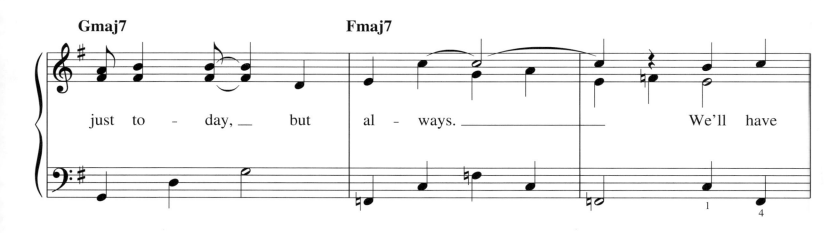

just to - day, ___ but al - ways. ___ We'll have

ear - ly morn-ing mad - ness, ___ we'll have mag - ic in the mak - ing. ___

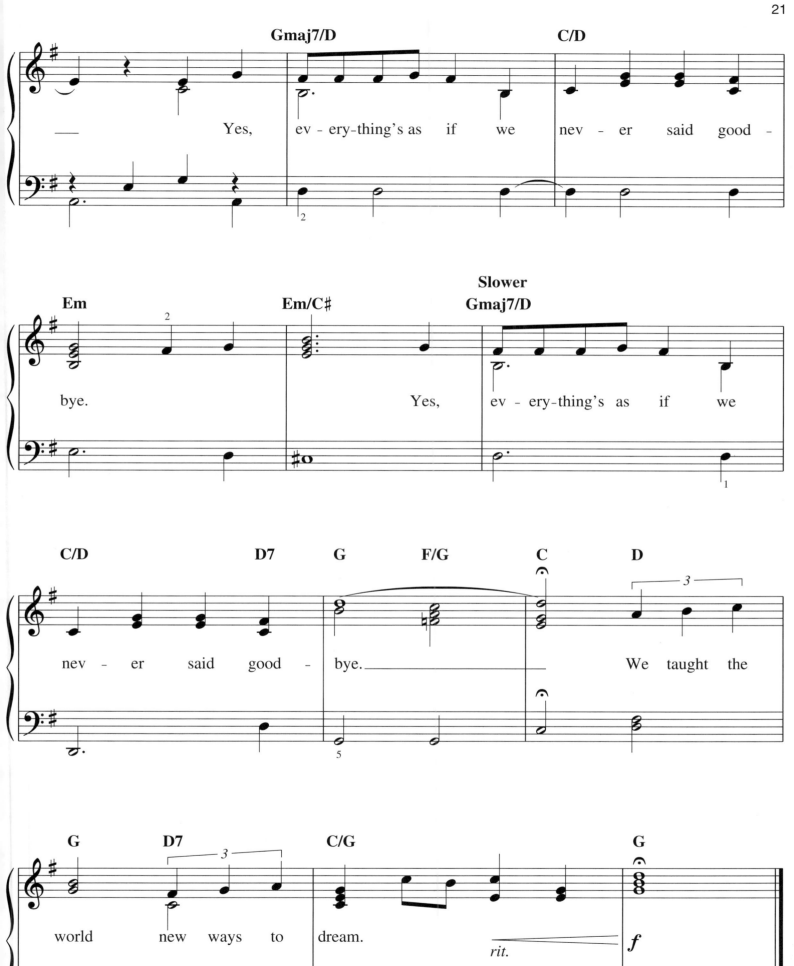

ANY DREAM WILL DO

from JOSEPH AND THE AMAZING TECHNICOLOR® DREAMCOAT

Music by ANDREW LLOYD WEBBER
Lyrics by TIM RICE

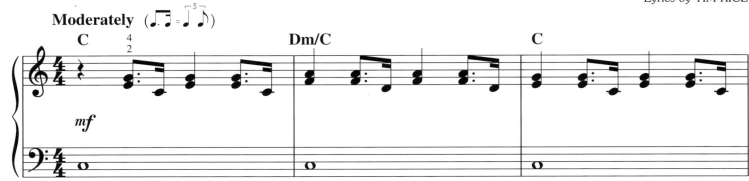

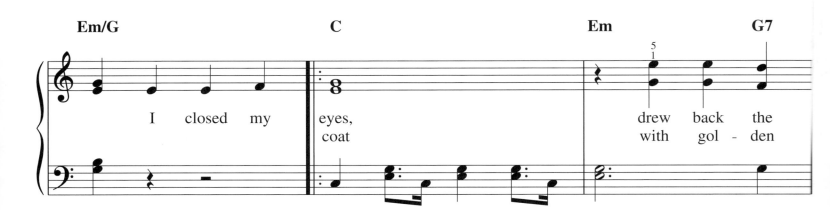

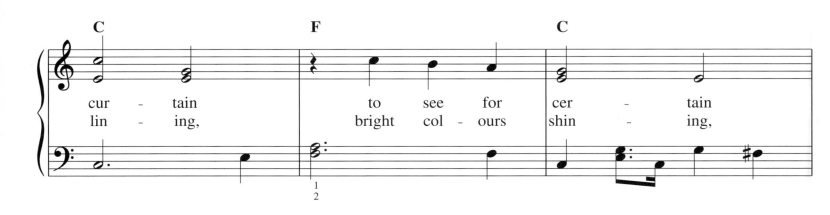

24

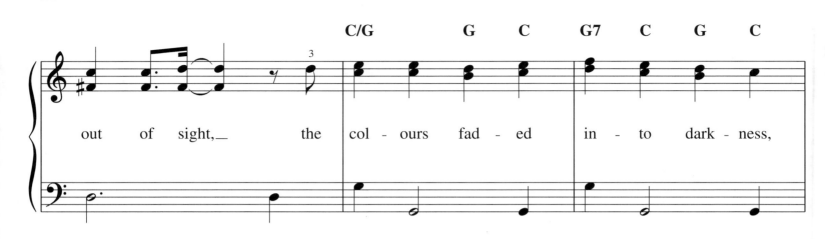

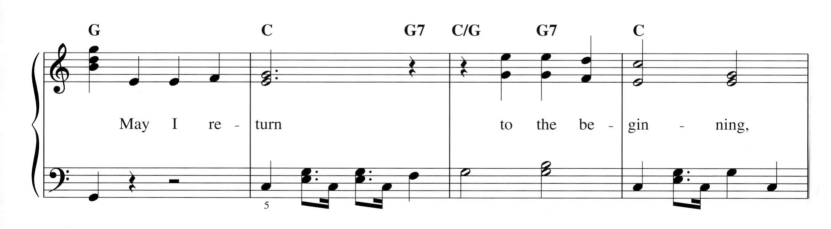

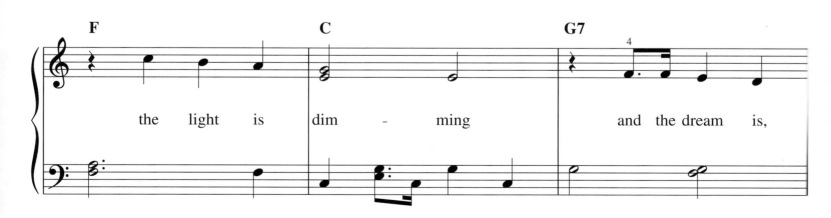

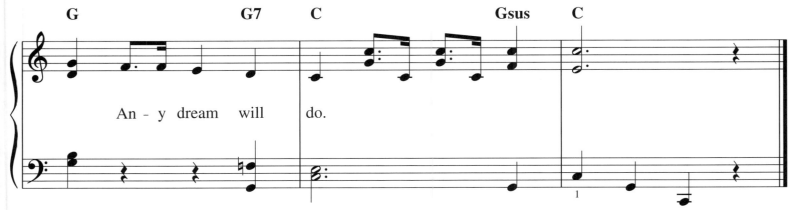

I BELIEVE MY HEART
from THE WOMAN IN WHITE

Music by ANDREW LLOYD WEBBER
Lyrics by DAVID ZIPPEL

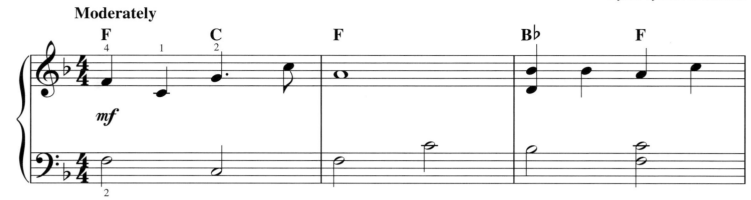

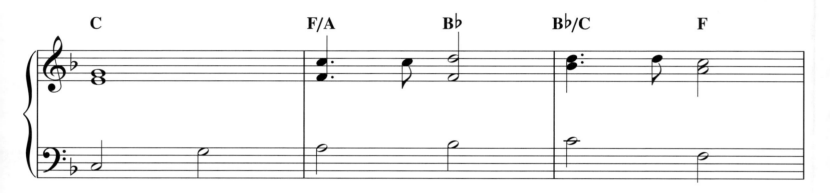

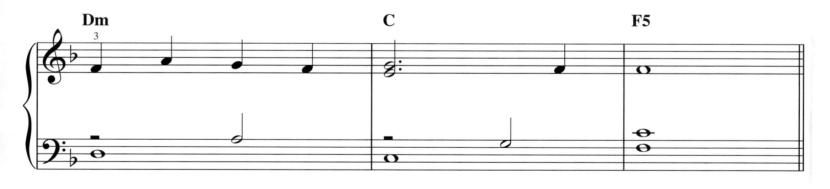

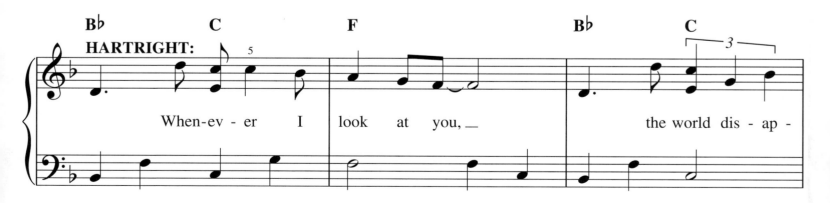

When-ev - er I look at you, _ the world dis - ap -

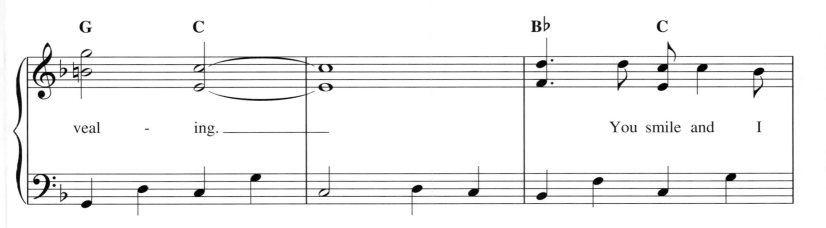

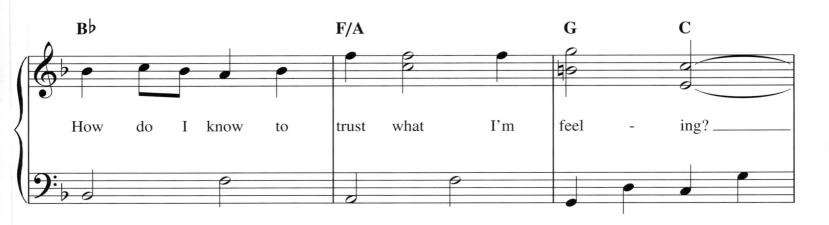

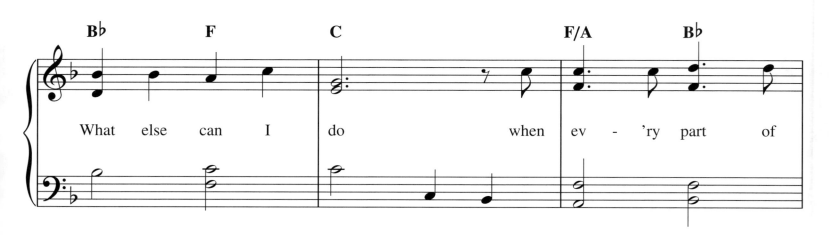

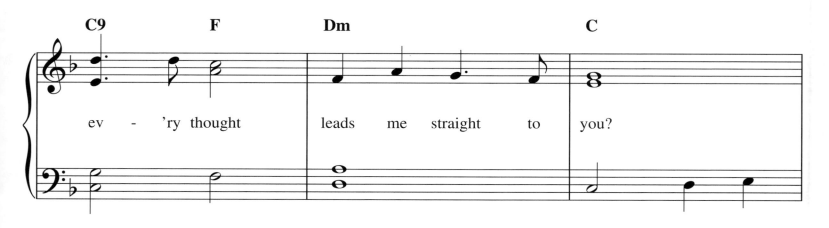

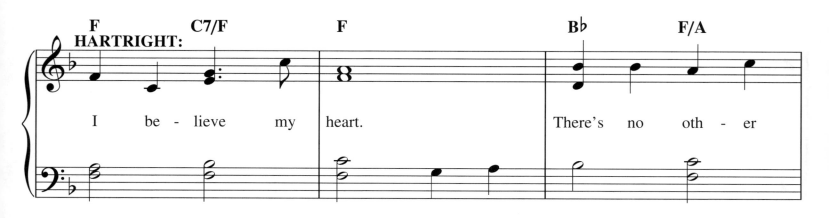

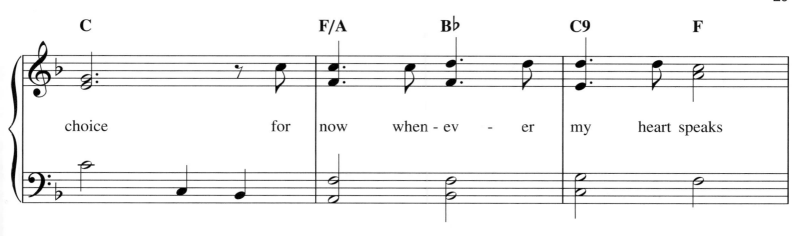

choice for now when - ev - er my heart speaks

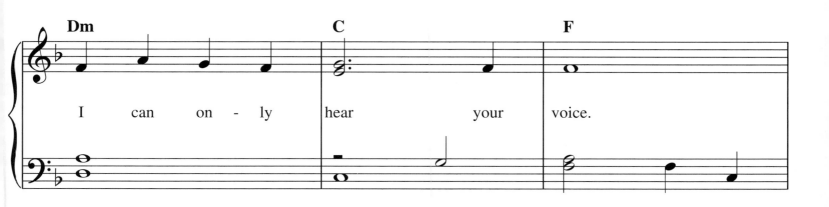

I can on - ly hear your voice.

LAURA: The life-time be - fore we met ___ has fad - ed a -

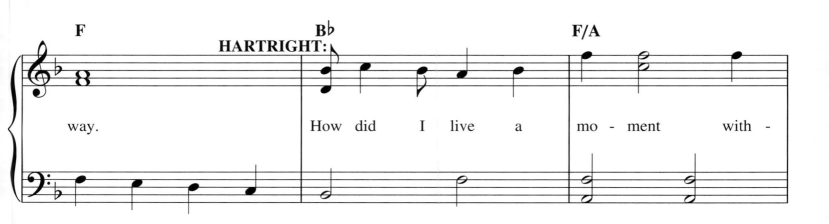

way. **HARTRIGHT:** How did I live a mo - ment with -

30

out   you? ___

LAURA:
You don't have to

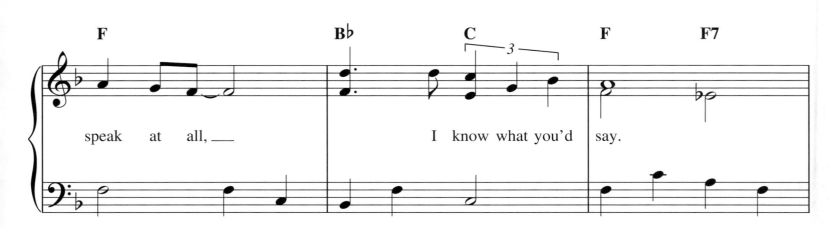

speak   at   all, ___

I know what you'd   say.

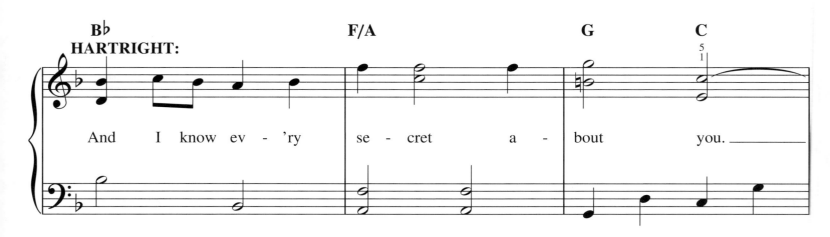

HARTRIGHT:
And   I know ev - 'ry   se - cret   a - bout   you. ___

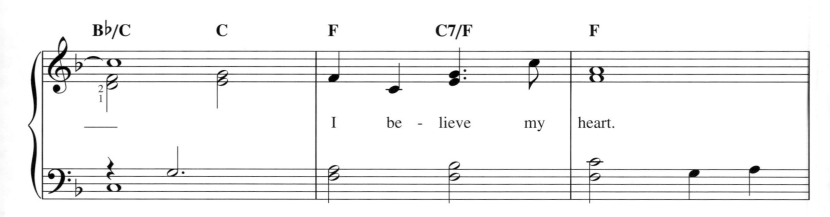

___   I be - lieve   my   heart.

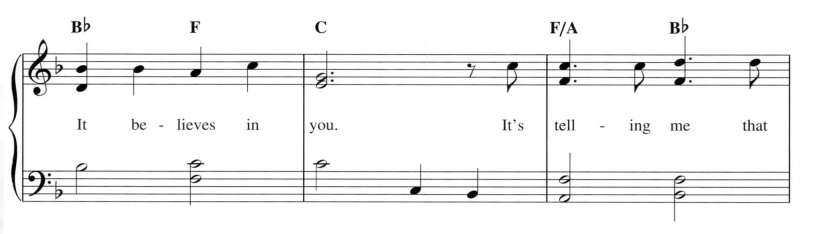

It be - lieves in you. It's tell - ing me that

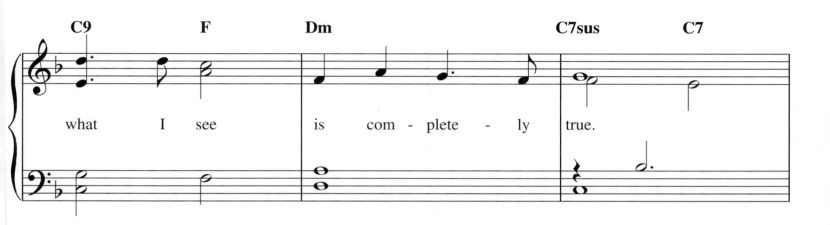

what I see is com - plete - ly true.

LAURA:
I be - lieve my heart. How can it be

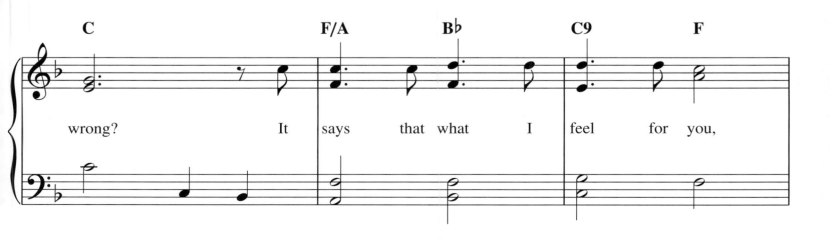

wrong? It says that what I feel for you,

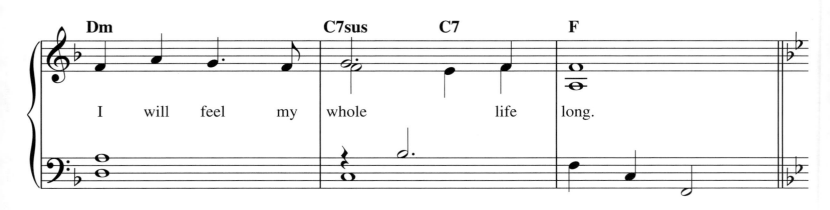

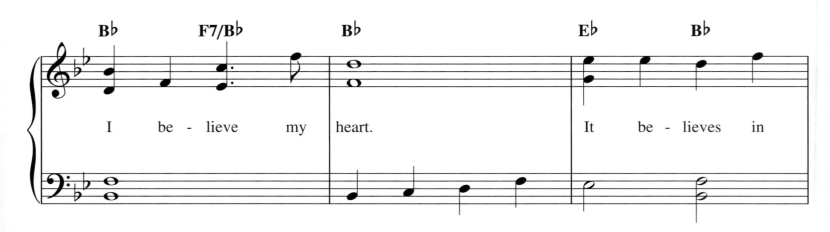

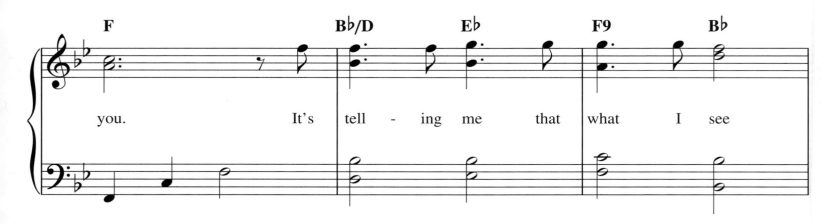

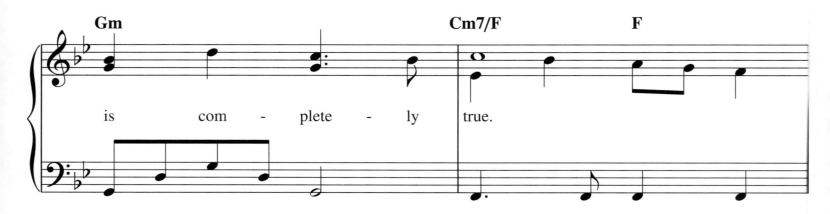

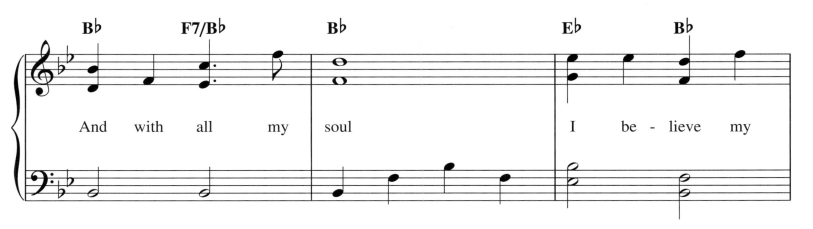

And with all my soul I be - lieve my

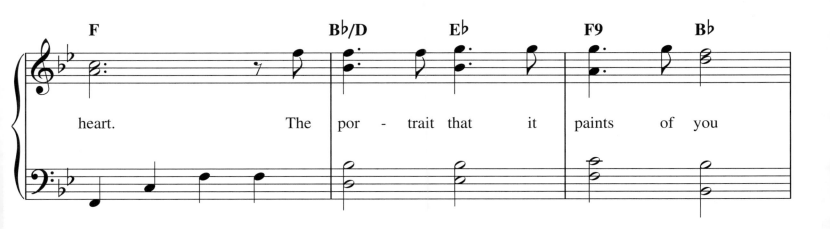

heart. The por - trait that it paints of you

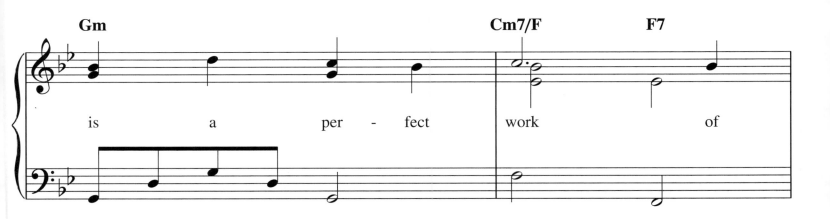

is a per - fect work of

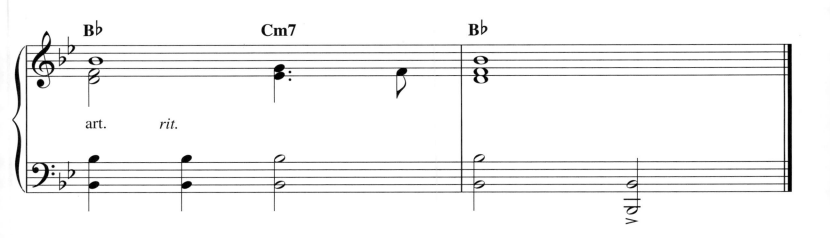

art. *rit.*

MEMORY
from CATS

Music by ANDREW LLOYD WEBBER
Text by TREVOR NUNN after T.S. ELIOT

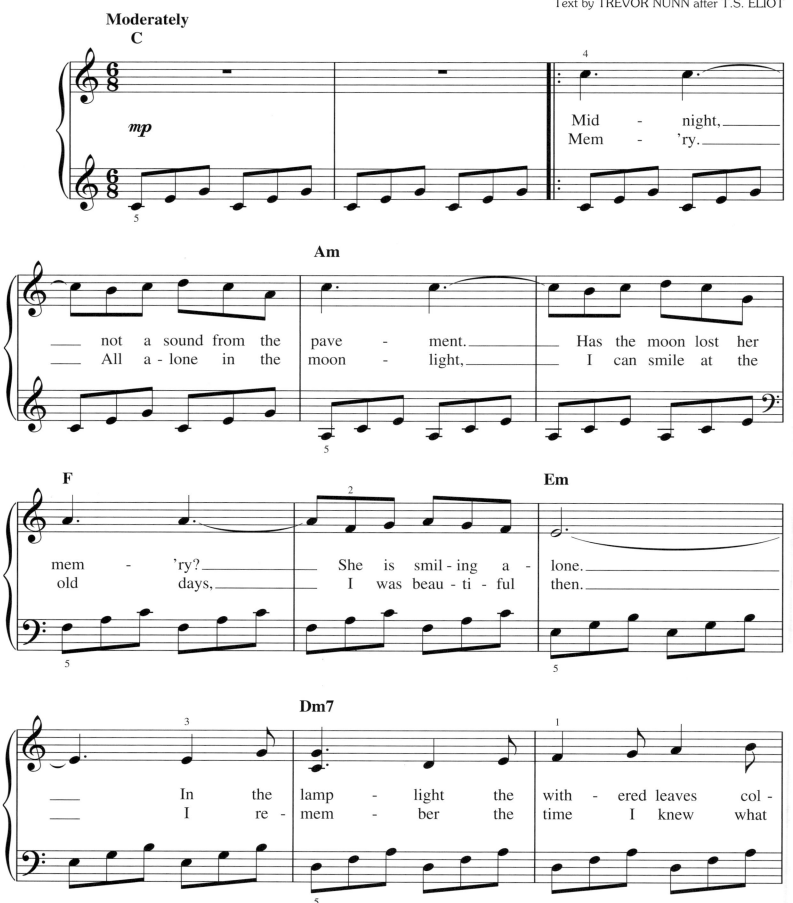

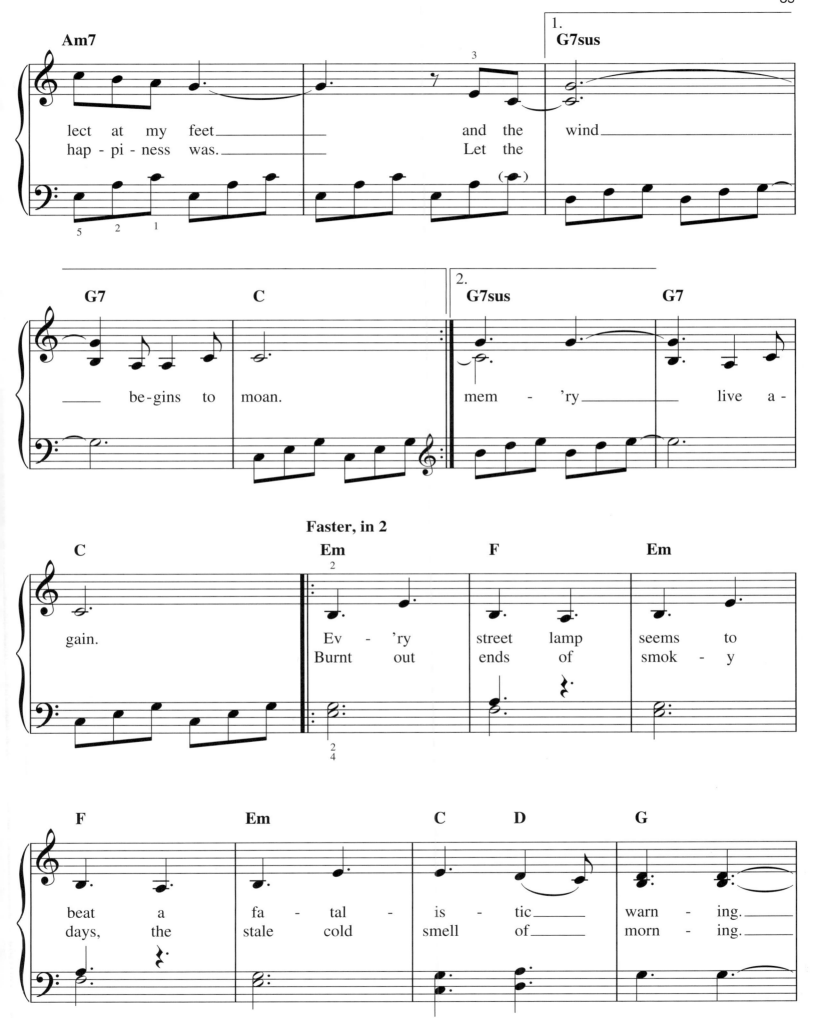

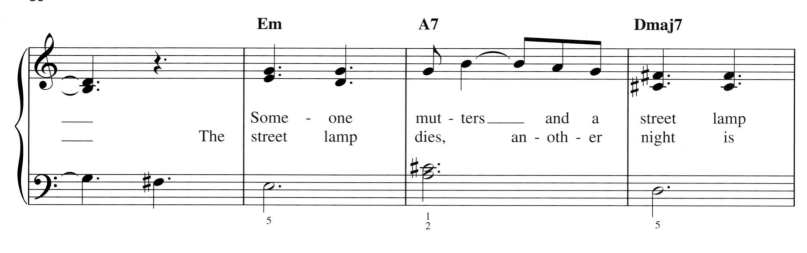

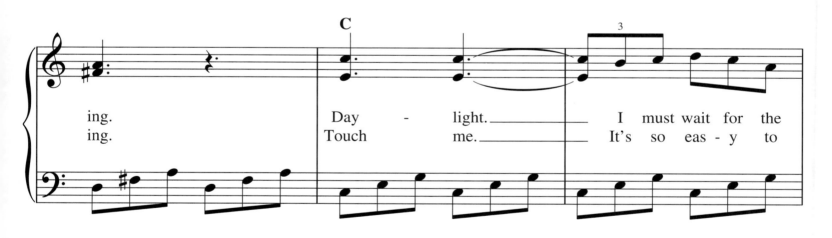

THINK OF ME

from THE PHANTOM OF THE OPERA

Music by ANDREW LLOYD WEBBER
Lyrics by CHARLES HART
Additional Lyrics by RICHARD STILGOE

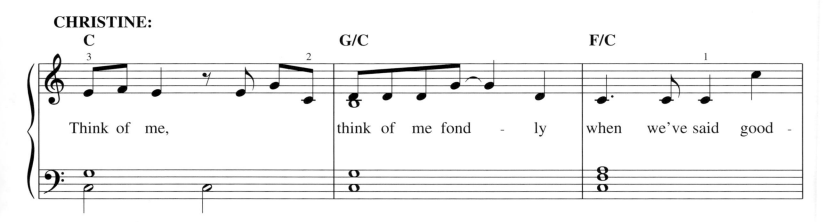

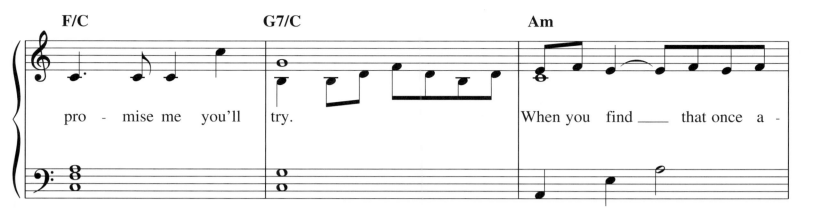

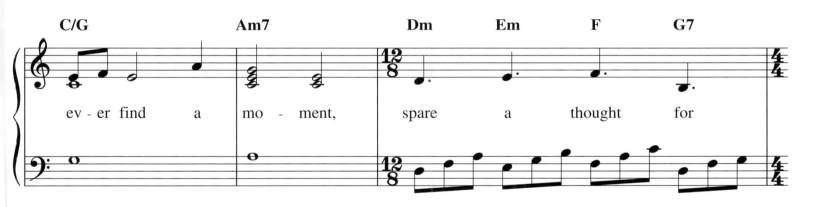

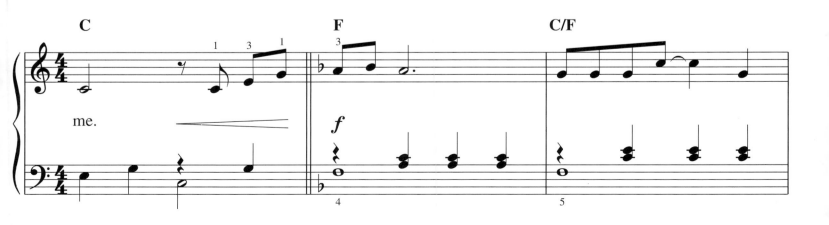

40

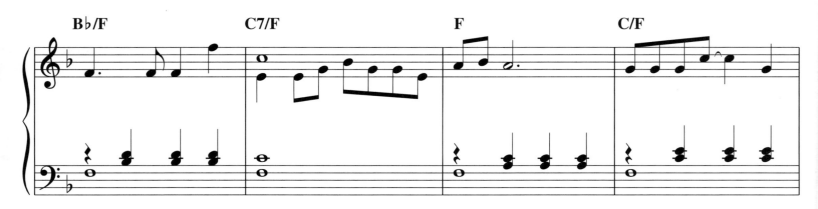

We nev - er said _____ our love was

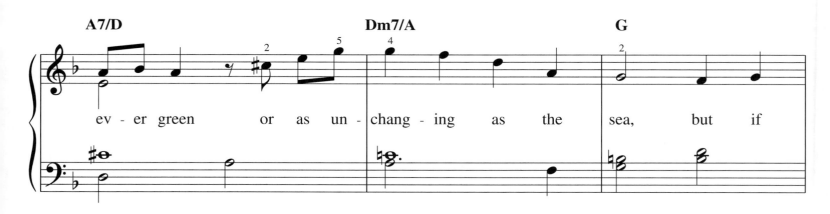

ev - er green   or   as un - chang - ing   as the   sea,   but if

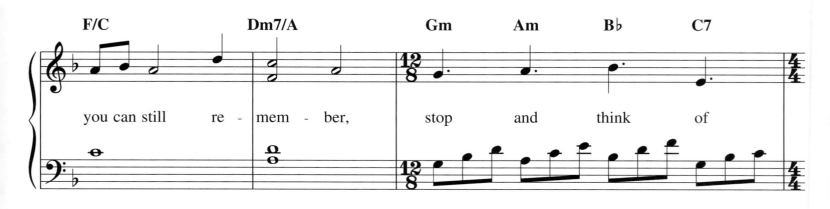

you can still re - mem - ber,   stop   and   think   of

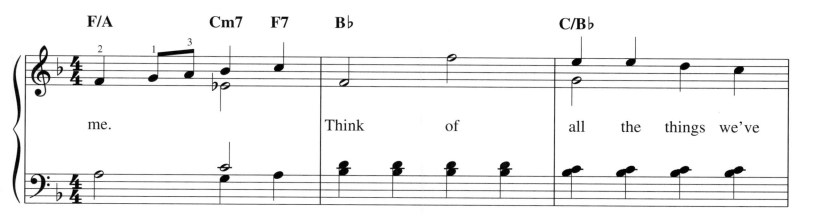

me. Think of all the things we've

shared and seen; don't think a - bout the

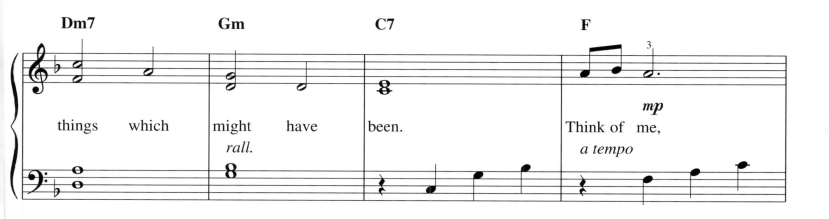

things which might have been. Think of me,

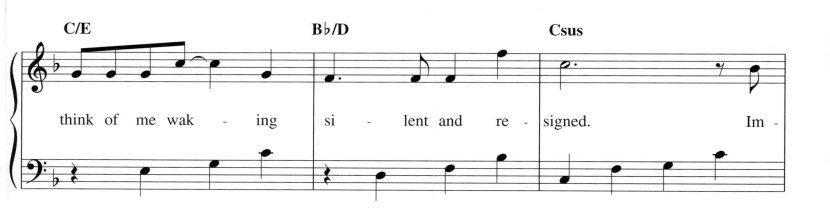

think of me wak - ing si - lent and re - signed. Im -

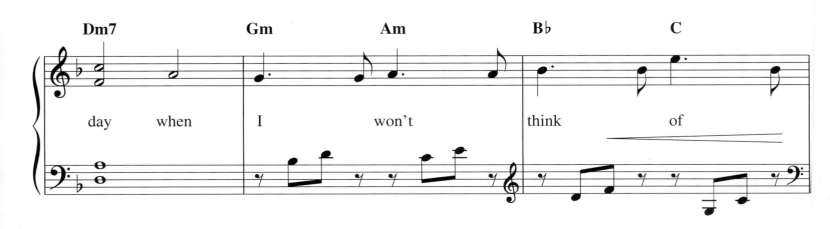

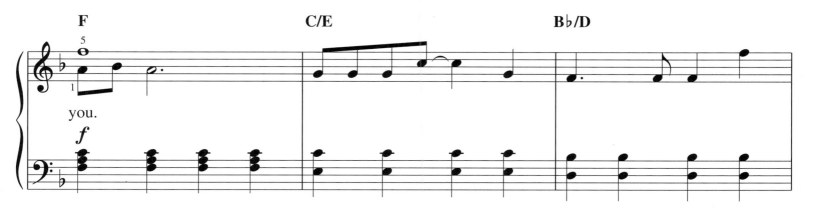

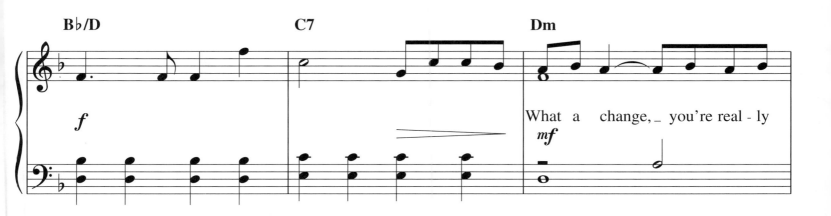

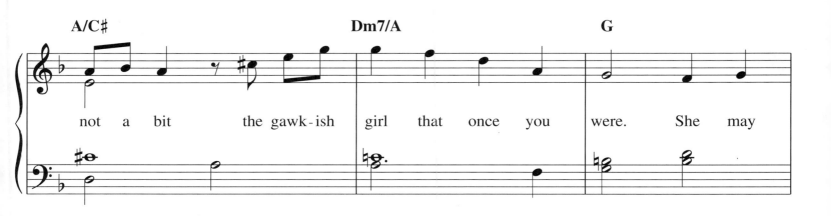

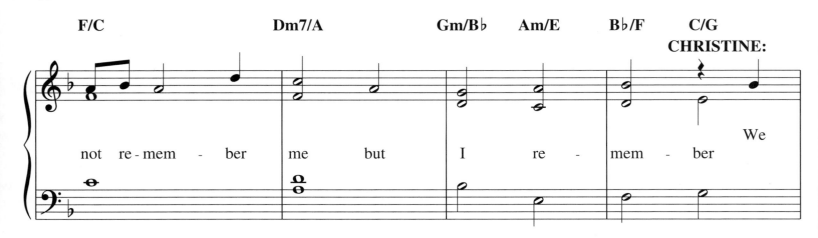

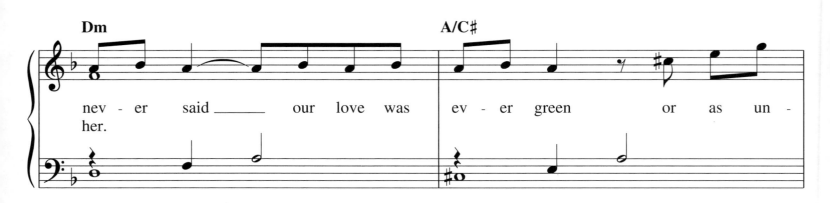

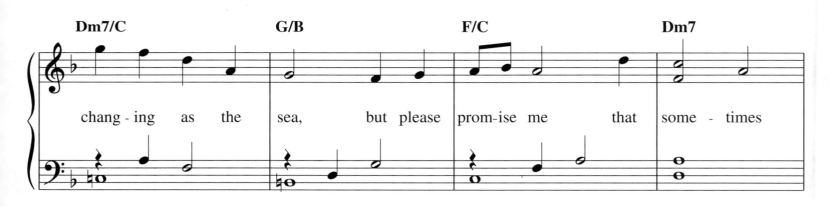

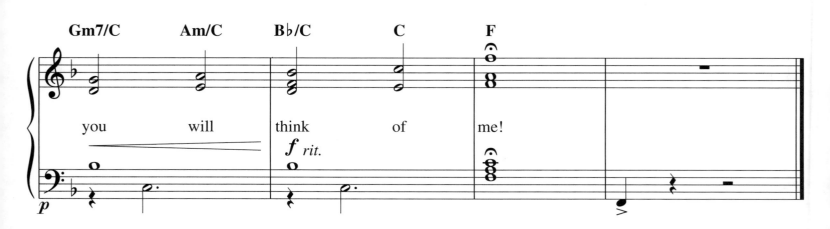

YOU MUST LOVE ME
from the Cinergi Motion Picture EVITA

Words by TIM RICE
Music by ANDREW LLOYD WEBBER

1. Where do we go from here?
2. (See additional lyrics)

This is-n't where we in-tend-ed to be. __ We had it all, __ you be-

lieved _ in me, __ I be- lieved _ in you. __

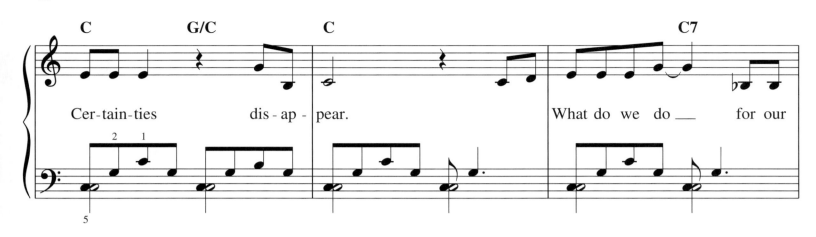

Cer-tain-ties   dis - ap - pear.   What do we do ___   for our

dream   to sur-vive,   how do we keep _   all our   pas-sions   a - live   as

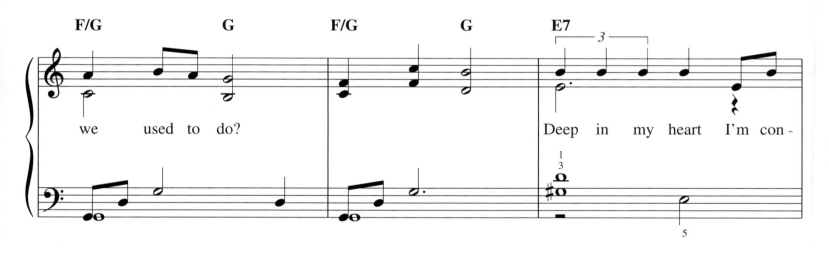

we   used to do?   Deep   in   my   heart   I'm con -

ceal - ing   things   that I'm long-ing   to   say,

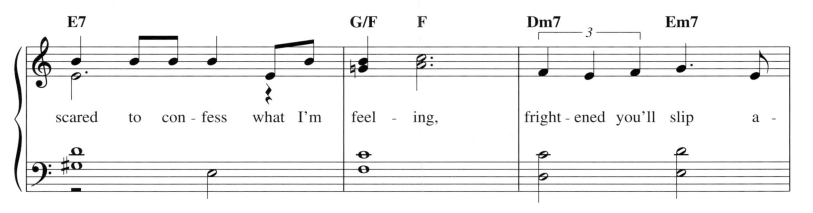

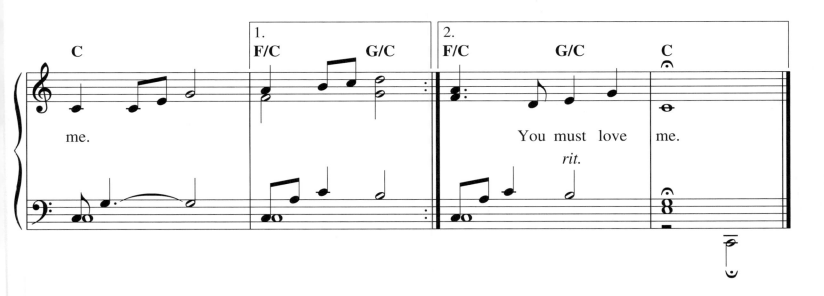

Additional Lyrics

2. *(Instrumental 8 bars)*
   Why are you at my side?
   How can I be any use to you now?
   Give me a chance and I'll let you see how
   Nothing has changed.
   Deep in my heart I'm concealing
   Things that I'm longing to say,
   Scared to confess what I'm feeling
   Frightened you'll slip away,
   You must love me.

UNEXPECTED SONG
from SONG & DANCE

Music by ANDREW LLOYD WEBBER
Lyrics by DON BLACK

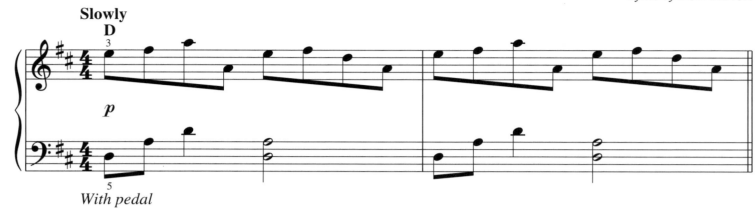

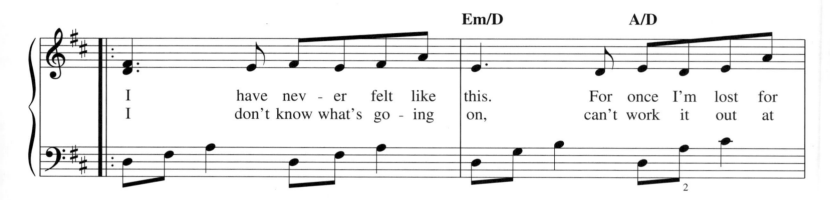

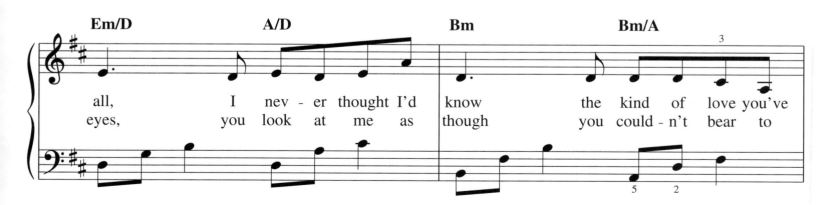

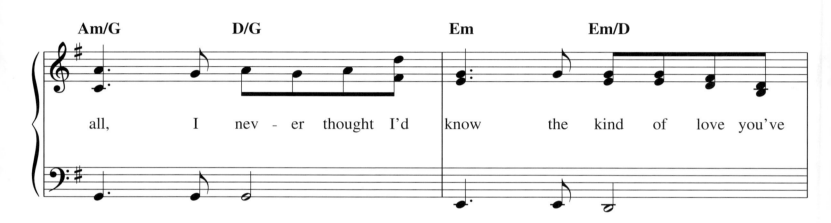

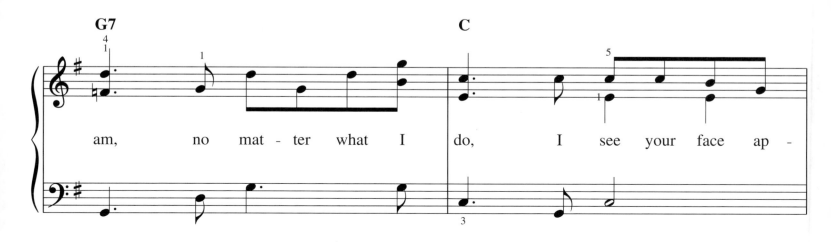

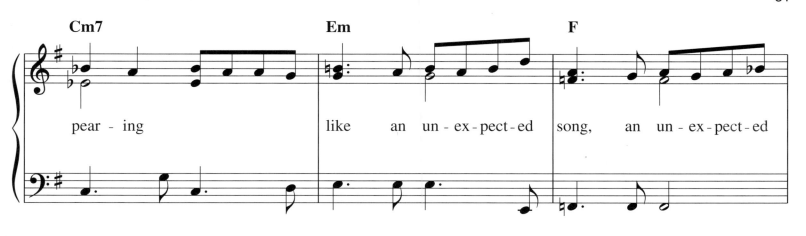

pear - ing   like   an un - ex - pect - ed   song,   an un - ex - pect - ed

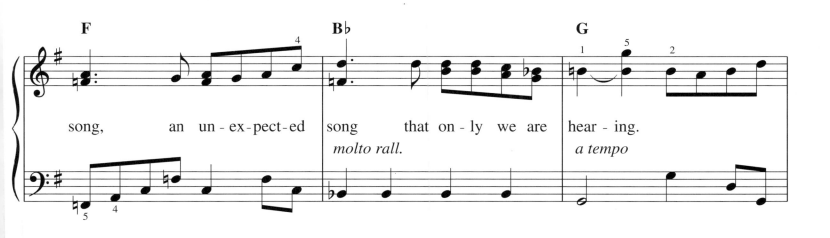

song   that on - ly we are   hear - ing.   Like   an un - ex - pect - ed

song,   an un - ex - pect - ed   song   that on - ly we are   hear - ing.

molto rall.   *a tempo*

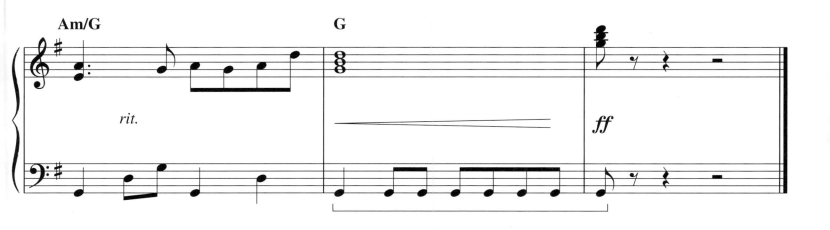

rit.   *ff*

WHISTLE DOWN THE WIND

from WHISTLE DOWN THE WIND

Music by ANDREW LLOYD WEBBER
Lyrics by JIM STEINMAN

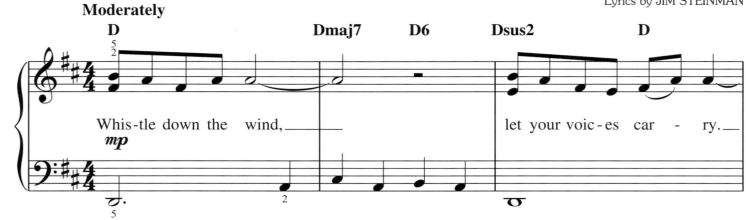

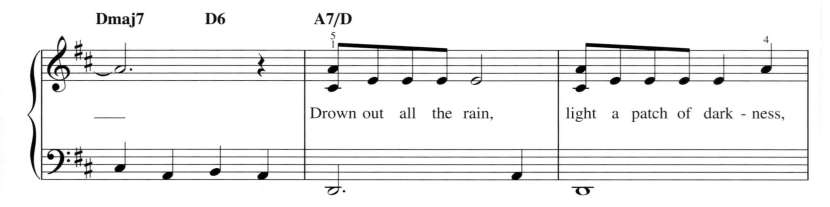

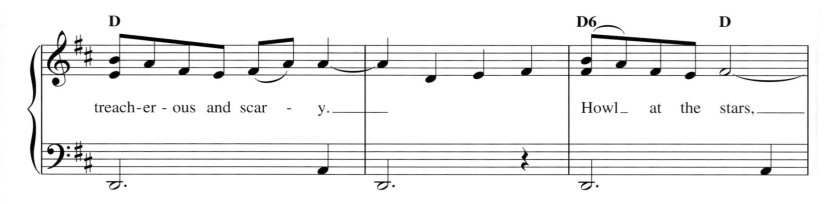

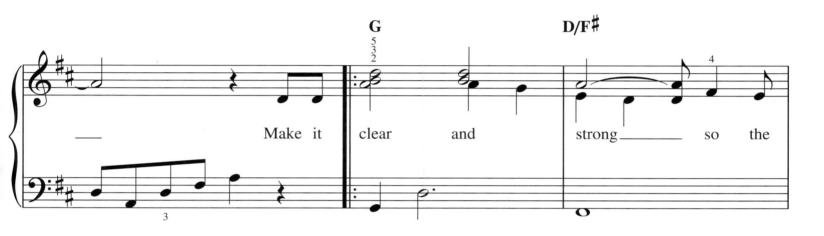

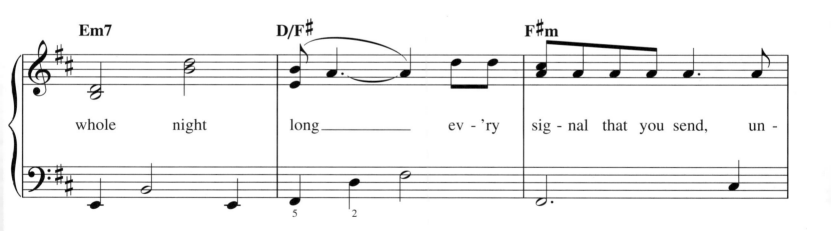

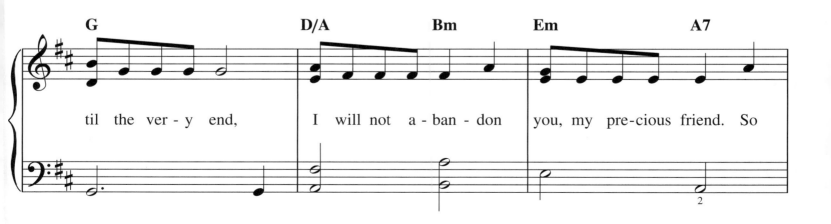

54

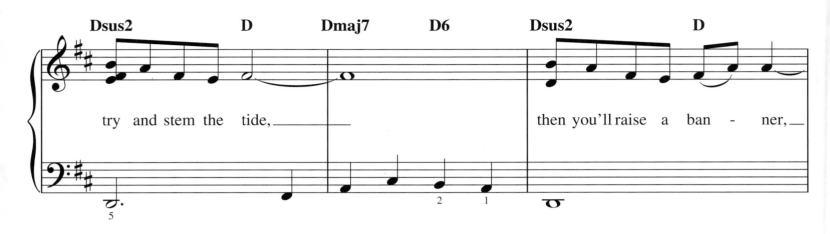

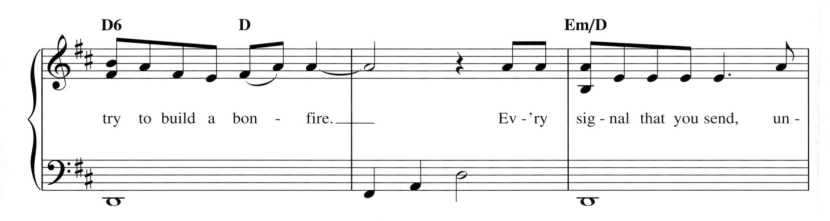

whis-tle down the wind,   for   I have al-ways been right   here._____

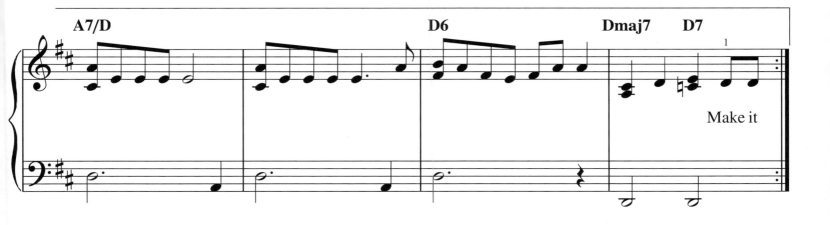

Make it

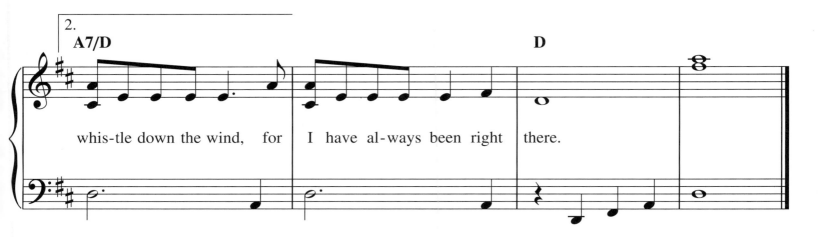

whis-tle down the wind,   for   I have al-ways been right   there.

EASY PIANO CD PLAY-ALONGS
Orchestrated arrangements with you as the soloist!

This series lets you play along with great accompaniments to songs you know and love! Each book comes with a CD of complete professional performances and includes matching custom arrangements in Easy Piano format. With these books you can: Listen to complete professional performances of each of the songs; Play the Easy Piano arrangements along with the performances; Sing along with the recordings; Play the Easy Piano arrangements as solos, without the CD.

GREAT JAZZ STANDARDS – VOLUME 1
Bewitched • Don't Get Around Much Anymore • How Deep Is the Ocean • It Might As Well Be Spring • My Funny Valentine • Satin Doll • Stardust • and more.
00310916 Easy Piano $14.95

FAVORITE CLASSICAL THEMES – VOLUME 2
Bach: Air on the G String • Beethoven: Symphony No. 5, Excerpt • Gounod: Ave Maria • Grieg: Morning • Handel: Hallelujah Chorus • Pachelbel: Canon • Tchaikovsky: Waltz of the Flowers • and more.
00310921 Easy Piano $14.95

BROADWAY FAVORITES – VOLUME 3
All I Ask of You • Beauty and the Beast • Bring Him Home • Cabaret • Close Every Door • I've Never Been in Love Before • If I Loved You • Memory • My Favorite Things • Some Enchanted Evening.
00310915 Easy Piano $14.95

ADULT CONTEMPORARY HITS – VOLUME 4
Amazed • Angel • Breathe • I Don't Want to Wait • I Hope You Dance • I Will Remember You • I'll Be • It's Your Love • The Power of Love • You'll Be in My Heart.
00310919 Easy Piano $14.95

HIT POP/ROCK BALLADS – VOLUME 5
Don't Let the Sun Go Down on Me • From a Distance • I Can't Make You Love Me • I'll Be There • Imagine • In My Room • Rainy Days and Mondays • Total Eclipse of the Heart • and more.
00310917 Easy Piano $14.95

LOVE SONG FAVORITES – VOLUME 6
Fields of Gold • I Honestly Love You • If • Lady in Red • More Than Words • Save the Best for Last • Three Times a Lady • Up Where We Belong • We've Only Just Begun • You Are So Beautiful.
00310918 Easy Piano $14.95

O HOLY NIGHT – VOLUME 7
Angels We Have Heard on High • God Rest Ye Merry, Gentlemen • It Came upon the Midnight Clear • O Holy Silent Night • What Child Is This? • and more.
00310920 Easy Piano $14.95

A CHRISTIAN WEDDING – VOLUME 8
Cherish the Treasure • Commitment Song • How Beautiful • I Will Be Here • In This Very Room • The Lord's Prayer • Love Will Be Our Home • Parent's Prayer • This Is the Day • The Wedding.
00311104 Easy Piano $14.95

COUNTRY BALLADS – VOLUME 9
Always on My Mind • Could I Have This Dance • Crazy • Crying • Forever and Ever, Amen • He Stopped Loving Her Today • I Can Love You Like That • The Keeper of the Stars • Release Me • When You Say Nothing at All.
00311105 Easy Piano $14.95

MOVIE GREATS – VOLUME 10
And All That Jazz • Chariots of Fire • Come What May • Forrest Gump • I Finally Found Someone • Iris • Mission: Impossible Theme • Tears in Heaven • There You'll Be • A Wink and a Smile.
00311106 Easy Piano $14.95

DISNEY BLOCKBUSTERS – VOLUME 11
Be Our Guest • Can You Feel the Love Tonight • Go the Distance • Look Through My Eyes • Reflection • Two Worlds • Under the Sea • A Whole New World • Written in the Stars • You've Got a Friend in Me.
00311107 Easy Piano $14.95

CHRISTMAS FAVORITES – VOLUME 12
Blue Christmas • Frosty the Snow Man • Here Comes Santa Claus • I'll Be Home for Christmas • Silver Bells • Wonderful Christmastime • and more.
00311257 Easy Piano $14.95

CHILDREN'S SONGS – VOLUME 13
Any Dream Will Do • Do-Re-Mi • It's a Small World • Linus and Lucy • The Rainbow Connection • Splish Splash • This Land Is Your Land • Winnie the Pooh • Yellow Submarine • Zip-A-Dee-Doo-Dah.
00311258 Easy Piano $14.95

CHILDREN'S FAVORITES – VOLUME 14
Alphabet Song • Frere Jacques • Home on the Range • My Bonnie Lies over the Ocean • Oh! Susanna • Old MacDonald • This Old Man • Yankee Doodle • and more.
00311259 Easy Piano $14.95

DISNEY'S BEST – VOLUME 15
Beauty and the Beast • Bibbidi-Bobbidi-Boo • Chim Chim Cher-ee • Colors of the Wind • Friend Like Me • Hakuna Matata • Part of Your World • Someday • When She Loved Me • You'll Be in My Heart.
00311260 Easy Piano $14.95

LENNON & McCARTNEY HITS – VOLUME 16
Eleanor Rigby • Hey Jude • The Long and Winding Road • Love Me Do • Lucy in the Sky with Diamonds • Nowhere Man • Please Please Me • Sgt. Pepper's Lonely Hearts Club Band • Strawberry Fields Forever • Yesterday.
00311262 Easy Piano $14.95

HOLIDAY HITS – VOLUME 17
Christmas Time Is Here • Feliz Navidad • I Saw Mommy Kissing Santa Claus • Jingle-Bell Rock • The Most Wonderful Time of the Year • My Favorite Things • Santa Claus Is Comin' to Town • and more.
00311329 Easy Piano $14.95

HIGH SCHOOL MUSICAL – VOLUME 18
Bop to the Top • Breaking Free • Get'cha Head in the Game • Stick to the Status Quo • We're All in This Together • What I've Been Looking For • When There Was Me and You • and more.
00311752 Easy Piano $14.95

HIGH SCHOOL MUSICAL 2 – VOLUME 19
All for One • Everyday • Fabulous • Gotta Go My Own Way • I Don't Dance • What Time Is It • Work This Out • You Are the Music in Me.
00311753 Easy Piano $14.95

ANDREW LLOYD WEBBER – FAVORITES – VOLUME 20
Another Suitcase in Another Hall • Any Dream Will Do • As If We Never Said Goodbye • I Believe My Heart • Memory • Think of Me • Unexpected Song • Whistle down the Wind • You Must Love Me • and more.
00311775 Easy Piano $14.95

GREAT CLASSICAL MELODIES – VOLUME 21
Arioso • Ave Maria • Fur Elise • Jesu, Joy of Man's Desiring • Lullaby (Cradle Song) • Meditation • Ode to Joy • Romeo and Juliet (Love Theme) • Sicilienne • Theme from Swan Lake • and more.
00311776 Easy Piano $14.95

ANDREW LLOYD WEBBER – HITS – VOLUME 22
Don't Cry for Me Argentina • I Don't Know How to Love Him • Love Changes Everything • The Music of the Night • No Matter What • Wishing You Were Somehow Here Again • With One Look • and more.
00311785 Easy Piano $14.95

Prices, contents and availability subject to change without notice.

FOR MORE INFORMATION, SEE YOUR LOCAL MUSIC DEALER, OR WRITE TO:

HAL•LEONARD®
CORPORATION
7777 W. BLUEMOUND RD. P.O. BOX 13819 MILWAUKEE, WI 53213

www.halleonard.com